Carry Me!

Animal Babies on the Move

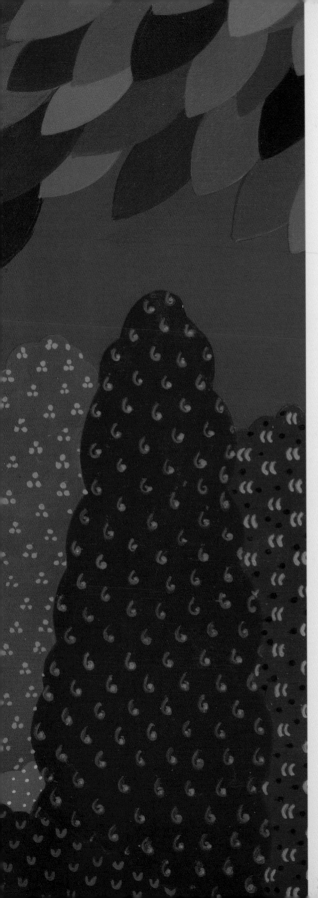

Dedication

To the loving memory of my mother, Abie Proudfoot

Acknowledgments

Special thanks to Dr. Robert Hoffmann, Dr. Stan Weitzman,
and Dr. Anna Weitzman of the National Museum of Natural History
and to Alvin Hutchinson of the National Zoological Park
for their helpful research assistance.

Published by
PEACHTREE PUBLISHERS
1700 Chattahoochee Avenue
Atlanta, Georgia 30318-2112

www.peachtree-online.com

ISBN 1-56145-328-5

Text and illustrations © 2005 by Susan Stockdale

Illustrations created in acrylic on paper. Text typeset in Adobe Optima.
Titles typeset in Apple Computer Techno.

Printed in Singapore
10 9 8 7 6 5 4 3 2 1
First Edition

Library of Congress Cataloging-in-Publication Data

Stockdale, Susan.
  Carry me! / written and illustrated by Susan Stockdale.— 1st ed.
      p. cm.
  ISBN 1-56145-328-5
  1. Parental behavior in animals—Juvenile literature. I. Title.
QL762.S74 2005
591.56'3—dc22

2004016585

Carry Me!

Animal Babies on the Move

Written and Illustrated by
Susan Stockdale

Ω

PEACHTREE
ATLANTA

Animals carry their young in all kinds of ways.

Riding on their backs

and clinging to their bellies.

Propped on their shoulders

and perched on their feet.

Carted on their tops

and braced beneath their wings.

Clutched to their breasts

and stretched across their chests.

Gripped in their teeth

and grasped in their jaws.

Tucked in their pouches

and gathered in their mouths.

Nestled in their feathers

and held in their arms.

Safe and snug,

the way your mother carried you.

Giant Anteater
Central and South America

Baboon
Africa

Golden Lion Tamarin
South America

Emperor Penguin
Antarctica

Wolf Spider
All parts of the world, except Antarctica

African Jacana
East, central, and southern Africa

Bat
All parts of the world, except
Antarctica and the Arctic

The Animals and Where They Live

Sea Otter

Pacific Ocean coast from California
north to Alaska; northeastern Siberia

Coyote

North and Central America

American Alligator

Southeastern United States

Kangaroo

Australia and New Guinea

African Cichlid

Central Africa

Great Crested Grebe

All parts of the world, except North
and South America and Antarctica

European Beaver

Northern Europe

These are just a few of the many books that I found helpful in developing the text and illustrations for **CARRY ME!**

ALL ABOUT ALLIGATORS by Jim Arnosky (Scholastic)

ANIMALS AND THEIR YOUNG by Malcolm Penny (Franklin Watts)

BEAVERS by Lynn Stone (Rourke Publishing)

THE BIRD ATLAS by Barbara Taylor (Dorling Kindersley Publisher)

COYOTE: NORTH AMERICA'S DOG by Stephen R. Swinburne (Boyds Mill Press)

FISH by Steve Parker (Dorling Kindersley Publisher)

HANGING ON: HOW ANIMALS CARRY THEIR YOUNG by Russell Freedman (Holiday House)

KANGAROOS by Denise Burt (Houghton Mifflin)

MONKEYS AND APES OF THE WORLD by Rita Golden Gelman (Franklin Watts)

OTTERS by Emilie U. Lepthien (Children's Press)

PENGUINS! by Gail Gibbons (Holiday House)

SPIDERS by Seymour Simon (HarperCollins Children's Books)

THOSE AMAZING BATS by Cheryl Halton (Dillon Press)

THE WONDERFUL WORLD OF YOUNG ANIMALS by Cathy Kilpatrick (The Hamlyn Publishing Group)

To Marc—I.M.

The author wishes to extend special
thanks to Art Matarazzo, Deputy Director,
Fire-Safety Education, New York City Fire
Department.

All artist's conceptions for fire trucks were
provided courtesy of the New York City
Fire Department except for the paintings of
early steam pumpers and fire engines, the
airport crash truck, and fireboats.

THE BIG BOOK OF REAL
FIRE TRUCKS
AND FIRE FIGHTING

by Teddy Slater
illustrated by Mones

BARNES
&NOBLE
BOOKS
NEW YORK

*F*ire fighting is one of the most dangerous jobs of all. Fire fighters risk their lives every day to save people and protect property. Fire fighters are hurt on their jobs more often than any other workers in the United States. And most fire departments in the United States today are volunteer departments, just like the first ones. These volunteer fire fighters have other jobs. When the alarm sounds they must leave their jobs and rush to the fire station. Paid fire departments are usually found in large cities. Paid departments have full-time fire fighters on duty round the clock at the station house.

Modern fire fighting departments are divided into two basic groups—engine companies and ladder companies. Engine companies use pumper trucks. Ladder companies use ladder trucks. Together the two companies race to a fire and work as a well-trained team.

One of the first pumper trucks was the horse-pulled steam pumper. Invented in the mid-1800s, it was a major improvement in fire fighting. Before that time, all pumpers had been powered by hand.

The First Fire Fighters

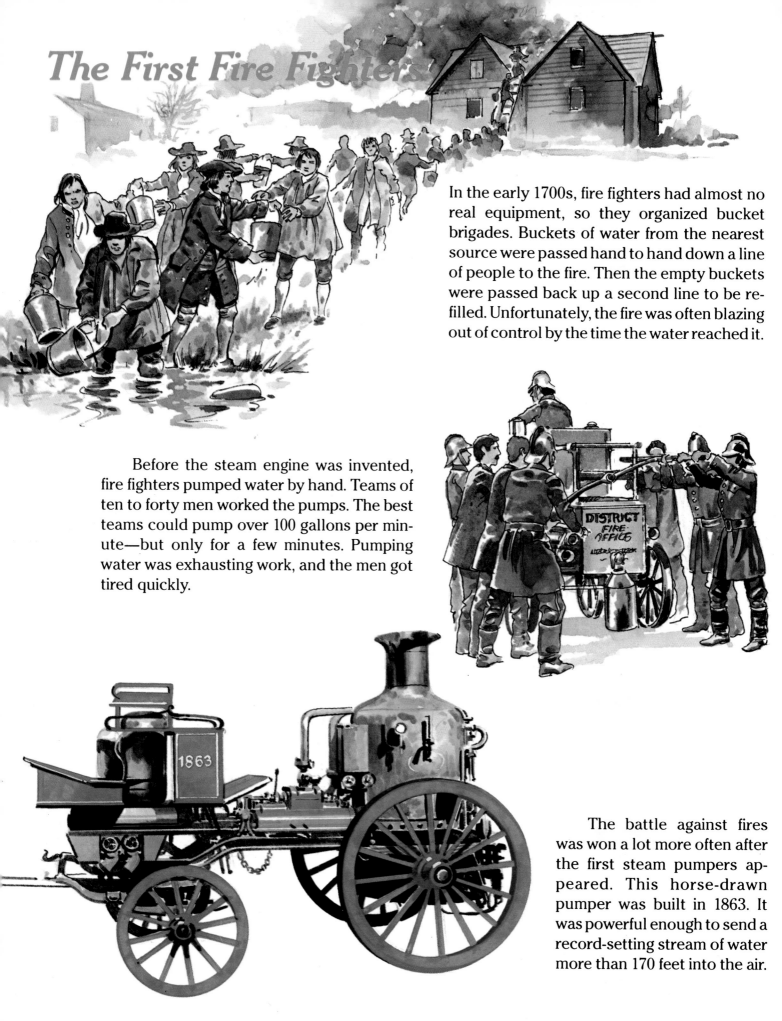

In the early 1700s, fire fighters had almost no real equipment, so they organized bucket brigades. Buckets of water from the nearest source were passed hand to hand down a line of people to the fire. Then the empty buckets were passed back up a second line to be re-filled. Unfortunately, the fire was often blazing out of control by the time the water reached it.

Before the steam engine was invented, fire fighters pumped water by hand. Teams of ten to forty men worked the pumps. The best teams could pump over 100 gallons per minute—but only for a few minutes. Pumping water was exhausting work, and the men got tired quickly.

The battle against fires was won a lot more often after the first steam pumpers appeared. This horse-drawn pumper was built in 1863. It was powerful enough to send a record-setting stream of water more than 170 feet into the air.

With this 1899 horse-pulled hook-and-ladder truck, firemen could climb into a burning building and rescue people. Of course there were no skyscrapers in those days, so the ladders didn't have to be very tall.

The first gasoline-engine fire truck was built in 1904. It had a powerful pump and carried an extension fire ladder, fire extinguishers, several hoses, and first-aid supplies.

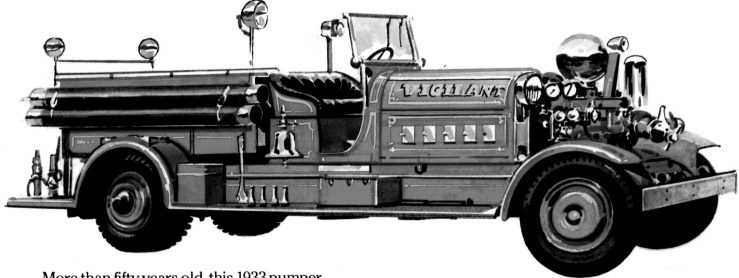

More than fifty years old, this 1933 pumper doesn't look very different from modern pumpers. But notice the open cab. As trucks got faster and faster, fire fighters had to remember to hang on so they wouldn't be thrown out of the truck.

The **Rear-Mount Aerial Ladder** is one of the most common trucks at a fire-fighting scene. The ladder can extend up to 100 feet, high enough for fire fighters to reach the top of any eight-story building. The last four or five feet of a fire ladder are always painted a bright color, usually yellow. Fire fighters can see the yellow ladder through the thick, black smoke near rooftops. The ladder sits on a small revolving table. It can turn the ladder in any direction. This truck also carries smaller, portable ladders, stretchers, first-aid equipment, and tools for breaking into buildings, such as crowbars, axes, sledgehammers, and saws.

Fire fighters on ladder trucks are responsible for people who might be trapped inside burning buildings. They must also ventilate the building by letting out the smoke and poisonous gases trapped inside. Fire fighters use their tools to break windows or cut holes in the walls and on the roof. If the gases are not let out, the heat and pressure inside can cause the building to explode.

The **Pumper** supplies the water for the fire fighters. The truck carries hoses, its own water tank, and a pump. There are inlet and outlet valves for hoses on both sides of the truck. Fire fighters use the valves on the side of the truck nearest to the hydrant. There are also hard, black hoses on the sides of the truck. These hoses are connected to the fire hydrant and then to inlet valves. The white canvas hoses are connected to the outlet valves. The pump inside the truck boosts the water's pressure before sending it out to the white canvas hoses.

The pumper can provide four hoses with 250 gallons of water per

minute—a total of 1,000 gallons. (Imagine taking forty baths to supply this truck with just one minute's worth of water!)

Many pumpers also have an additional small hose wound on a reel. This hose is called a booster line. Fire fighters use this hose to put out small fires outdoors.

Fire fighters on this truck are responsible for making sure the fire doesn't spread. Sometimes they spray water on nearby buildings that could be in danger of catching fire. Then they turn the hoses on the fire until it is out.

The **Hose Wagon** is very useful, sort of a combination pumper and rescue truck. The hose wagon only goes out on really big fires where extra hoses might be needed. Besides carrying hoses in many different sizes, the truck carries extra nozzles, a booster tank of water, and some first-aid equipment.

What Fire Fighters Wear

Fire fighters have to be very strong to put out fires. They must also be very strong just to put on their clothes. The helmet weighs 4 pounds; the coat, 7 pounds; and each boot, 3 pounds. Fire fighters carry an air tank and face mask that together weigh 27 pounds. Plus, there are about 10 pounds of small tools in a fire fighter's pockets. After dressing, a fire fighter wears more than 75 pounds of protective clothing and gear. That is about the weight of the average nine- or ten-year-old reading this book!

Sometimes fire fighters have to walk right through flames. Then they wear special suits that cover every inch of their bodies, from head to toe. The suits are fireproof and have a special aluminum coating that reflects the heat—and makes fire fighters look like astronauts.

The **Tiller Rig** is actually two separate vehicles joined together like a tractor trailer. It takes two people to drive this long ladder truck. The person who drives the front part is called the chauffeur. The person who steers the back part is the tillerman. The two drivers can make the front and rear wheels go in two different directions at the same time.

Like other ladder trucks, the tiller rig carries portable ladders and forcible entry tools. This truck is especially useful for turning sharp corners and for traveling through crowded, big-city streets.

The **Tower Ladder** or **Snorkel Truck** does not really have a ladder. It has a crane or boom. Instead of climbing a ladder, fire fighters ride inside a bucket or platform at the end of the boom. The bucket is lifted hydraulically and takes fire fighters up or down from a burning building. The bucket is large enough for seven people. The boom sits on a turntable so it can turn in any direction.

On large trucks, the boom can extend 150 feet. Supporting jacks help secure the truck when the boom is extended. A built-in hose runs the length of the boom. This hose is used to help put out fires. The tower ladder is perfect for people who may be too badly injured or too frightened to make their way down a ladder.

The **Fire Chief's Car** is usually red. When the chief hurries to a fire, the lights on the roof flash, and the siren blares. All other cars on the road must pull over to the side, out of the way, until the chief goes by. The chief is always at the biggest fires. The chief's car is equipped with a special telephone and two-way radio so the chief can stay in touch with headquarters and with fire fighters at the scene of the fire, too.

Who's Who at a Fire

Here are just a few of the people you would be likely to see at a big fire. Many of their names date back to the time when all fire fighters were men. The names have stayed the same even though women are now part of many fire fighting teams.

The *Chauffeur* is the ladder truck driver. He or she must park the truck as close to the fire as possible.

The pumper driver is known as the *MPO (Motor Pump Operator)*. The MPO must get water to the fire and is in charge of hooking up the hoses to the hydrant and regulating the flow of water to each hose.

The *Can Man* carries the fire extinguisher (nicknamed "the can"). A Can Man must be very strong, because the can weighs about 30 pounds.

The *Roof Man* rushes straight to the top of the building as soon as he or she arrives at the fire. If necessary, the Roof Man makes a hole in the roof so that smoke and heat can escape to prevent an explosion.

The *Outside Vent Man* goes to the back of the building, opens the windows, and crawls inside to make sure no one is trapped inside the building.

Several fire fighters must hold the hose because the water pressure is very high. If the hose were turned loose, it would jerk wildly all over the street. The person closest to the nozzle is known as the *Nozzle Man.*

The *Fire Chief* controls the whole operation. Each company at the scene has an officer who reports to the Fire Chief.

The *Dalmation* is the fire department's unofficial mascot or good luck charm. This friendly dog became the firehouse mascot because it was the only breed that could get along with the horses that pulled the early fire engines.

The **Rescue Van** and the fire fighters who ride inside are called the rescue company. A rescue company is seen at major fires and assists the ladder company. Sometimes the fire fighters are called rescue workers because they handle all kinds of emergencies, not just fires. They might, for example, be called to rescue an accident victim trapped inside or underneath a smashed car.

The rescue van carries all kinds of equipment and tools for fire fighting and emergencies. The workers receive special training so they can use all the equipment in their truck. Their equipment includes forcible entry tools, special suits for walking through fire, scuba gear for underwater rescues, and lifesaving medical equipment.

PIKE POLE

AX

SLEDGE HAMMER

CROW BAR

FIRE
EXTINGUISHER

ROPE

SCUBA-DIVING
EQUIPMENT

FIRST-AID KIT

BOLT CUTTERS

SMOKE EJECTOR

POWER SAW

AIR CYLINDER AND MASK

The **Foam Unit** is a big pumper that puts out fires with a special liquid that comes out like foam. This truck is used mostly for oil fires. Because foam cannot be shot high into the air like water, this truck has a long boom with a nozzle at the end. The boom can extend above the tallest oil tank and spray foam all over the tank to smother any flames.

Whenever an airplane accident occurs, the **Airport Crash Truck** rushes to the site and begins rescue operations immediately. The huge crash truck is built for speed so it can reach an airplane in seconds. The tires on a crash truck are designed to have good traction. All the tires stay on the ground even when it is rough and bumpy. The truck carries its own supply of water (about 1,000 gallons), dry chemicals, and a large pump. The water and chemicals mix together and make a foam that can put out fires involving jet fuel, gasoline, and other highly explosive materials. The foam is shot out of the cannon-like nozzles on the top and front of the cab. Some trucks have additional nozzles on the sides. Fire fighters often wear heat- and flame-proof suits for airport fires.

A Night at the Firehouse

The fire department is on the alert twenty-four hours a day. That is why fire fighters work in shifts. Some spend their days at the firehouse or station. Some spend their nights.

1. At 6:00 PM, Pete, a fire fighter, checks in at the fire station to work the night shift.

2. Pete goes upstairs to his locker and changes into his work clothes. He must be ready to go as soon as an alarm sounds.

3. Then Pete waits with other fire fighters until an alarm comes in. To pass the time, the fire fighters watch television, read, and eat dinner together.

4. Someone reports a fire, and a bell clangs in the firehouse.

5. Pete and the other fire fighters race to the pole and slide down to the ground floor. This is quicker than taking the stairs.

6. In less than a minute, Pete puts on his protective clothing. He is ready to go.

7. With sirens blaring, the fire trucks speed away from the station.

8. All the fire fighters work together to put out the fire. Then they return to the firehouse.

9. But their work isn't over yet. At the station, the fire fighters clean the fire trucks. They replace used hoses with fresh, dry ones. Now the trucks are ready for the next fire.

10. Other fire fighters clean the used hoses. Then the hoses are hung up to dry.

11. Pete and the other fire fighters settle down again to pass the time until the next alarm sounds.

12. Early the next morning, Pete leaves the firehouse. It has been a long night. As Pete goes home to get some sleep, a day-shift fire fighter comes in to take his place.

The **Mobile Headquarters Unit** serves as a command station for the biggest fires in large cities. The unit is operated by some of the highest-ranking officers in the fire department. From mobile headquarters, officers can organize the complicated efforts of the many fire fighters battling the blaze. The truck carries radio equipment as well as the floor plans for

every tall building and skyscraper in the area. The floor plans show all the doors, windows, fire exits, and sprinkler systems in the burning building. By studying the plans, officers can tell the fire fighters exactly where they should go. The officers use their radio equipment to talk to the fire fighters without ever having to leave mobile headquarters.

The **Brush-Fire Unit** is a special truck used in the country and in out-of-the-way places where there aren't any fire hydrants or local water sources such as lakes or rivers. The truck carries its own water supply, a long hose, shovels, and rakes. Small grass and brush fires can be fought without the aid of other fire trucks. The brush-fire unit is a rugged little truck with four-wheel drive, just like a jeep. It can travel deep into the woods and over the wildest, wettest land without getting stuck.

The **Searchlight Unit** is used at the biggest, blackest fires. It is always pretty dark in the middle of a fire. Ladder trucks even carry their own lights and power generators. But for some really smoky fires, where more light is needed, fire fighters use this special searchlight truck. It has eight

super spotlights. They don't look very big. But when all eight spotlights are lit, they provide enough power to light up Yankee Stadium for a night baseball game!

Fireboats fight fires in waterfront buildings and on ships and piers. These boats don't need any hydrants or booster tanks of water. Each boat has its own giant pump that sucks up water directly from rivers, lakes, or oceans. There is no limit to the amount of water fireboats can use. A big nozzle shoots the water directly onto the fire. Some huge fireboats can pump as much as 22,000 gallons of water per minute! That's equal to about nine pumper trucks put together.

How a Fire Alarm Work

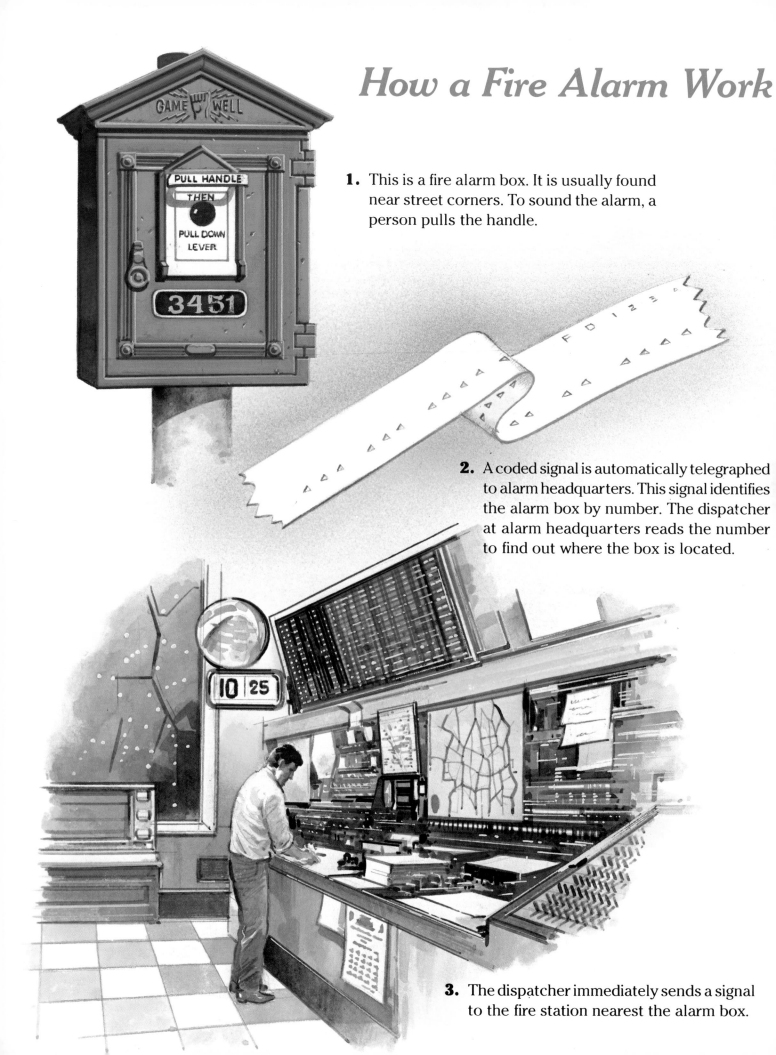

1. This is a fire alarm box. It is usually found near street corners. To sound the alarm, a person pulls the handle.

2. A coded signal is automatically telegraphed to alarm headquarters. This signal identifies the alarm box by number. The dispatcher at alarm headquarters reads the number to find out where the box is located.

3. The dispatcher immediately sends a signal to the fire station nearest the alarm box.

4. Fire fighters go directly to the alarm box. The person who sent in the alarm should be waiting there to show fire fighters where to go.

5. If the fire is a big one, the fire fighters will call in another alarm. The dispatcher will send out a message to another fire station for more trucks. This is called a two-alarm fire. Each alarm means more trucks will rush to the fire.

6. New alarm boxes in many parts of the country have telephones or two-way radios. The person reporting a fire can talk directly to the dispatcher.

What a terrible fire! Many of the trucks pictured in this book are needed to handle this fire. Also on hand is a **Paramedic Unit**. The fire fighters in the paramedic unit are specially trained to give on-the-spot medical care. This truck, sometimes called an ambulance, carries medical equipment and has a two-way radio for contact with a hospital nearby. Besides the paramedic unit, how many fire trucks can you name?